20 THINGS YOU DIDN'T KNOW ABOUT

HOCKEY

THEIA LAKE

PowerKiDS press

Published in 2026 by The Rosen Publishing Group, Inc.
2544 Clinton Street, Buffalo, NY 14224

Portions of this work were originally authored by Ryan Nagelhout and published as *20 Fun Facts About Hockey*. All new material in this edition was authored by Theia Lake.

Editor: Greg Roza
Book Design: Tanya Dellaccio Keeney

Photo Credits: Cover Master1305/Shutterstock.com; p. 5 Historic Collection/Alamy Images; p. 6 https://upload.wikimedia.org/wikipedia/commons/9/9a/1910_Ice_Hockey_European_Championships_-_Berlin_vs_Brussels.jpg; p. 7 Erik Clegg/Shutterstock.com; p. 8 https://upload.wikimedia.org/wikipedia/commons/6/65/Mikmac-hockey-sticks.jpg; p. 9 Robert Nyholm/Shutterstock.com; p. 10 https://upload.wikimedia.org/wikipedia/commons/d/da/Skating_Carnival%2C_Victoria_Rink%2C_Montreal%2C_QC%2C_painted_composite%2C_1870.jpg; p. 11 Pictures Now/Alamy Images; p. 12 (left) Tatohra/Shutterstock.com; p. 12 (right) Michael715/Shutterstock.com; p. 13 Neftali/Alamy Images; pp. 14, 16 UPI/Alamy Images; p. 15 Dave Pattinson/Alamy Images; p. 17 Shutterstock AI Generator/Shutterstock.com; p. 18 The Macomb Daily/AP Images; p. 19 Jason O. Watson (Sports)/Alamy Images; p. 20 https://upload.wikimedia.org/wikipedia/commons/0/01/Plante_Mask.jpg; p. 21 tony quinn/Alamy Images; p. 22 Rudmer Zwerver /Shutterstock.com; p. 23 Cal Sport Media/Alamy Images; p. 24 https://upload.wikimedia.org/wikipedia/commons/2/25/First_Stanley_Cup.jpg; p. 25 4kclips/Shutterstock.com; p. 26 Adwo/Shutterstock.com; p. 27 Klara_Steffkova/Shutterstock.com; p. 29 MediaPunch Inc/Alamy Images.

Some of the images in this book illustrate individuals who are models. The depictions do not imply actual situations or events.

Library of Congress Cataloging-in-Publication Data
Names: Lake, Theia, author.
Title: 20 things you didn't know about hockey / Theia Lake.
Other titles: Twenty things you didn't know about hockey
Description: Buffalo, New York : PowerKids Press, [2026] | Series: Did you know? Sports | Includes index.
Identifiers: LCCN 2025002329 (print) | LCCN 2025002330 (ebook) | ISBN 9781499450392 (lib. bdg.) | ISBN 9781499450385 (paperback) | ISBN 9781499450408 (ebook)
Subjects: LCSH: Hockey–Miscellanea–Juvenile literature. | Hockey–History–Juvenile literature.
Classification: LCC GV847.25 .L35 2026 (print) | LCC GV847.25 (ebook) | DDC 796.962-dc23/eng/20250202
LC record available at https://lccn.loc.gov/2025002329
LC ebook record available at https://lccn.loc.gov/2025002330

Manufactured in the United States of America

CPSIA Compliance Information: Batch #CSPK26. For Further Information contact Rosen Publishing at 1-800-237-9932.

CONTENTS

HIT THE ICE!

Hockey is one of the most popular sports in the world, and it's particularly popular in North America. You might play roller or floor hockey with your friends, but the game was originally played on iced-over ponds and indoor ice rinks. Hockey is fast, fun, and full of interesting facts.

Big shots and even bigger saves highlight a game filled with heroes known as "The Great One" and "The Dominator." Want to learn more? Then grab your skates and hit the ice!

Hockey players love to give each other fun nicknames. One of the greatest players in history, Montreal's Maurice Richard, was called the "Rocket" when he hit the ice!

PASS THE PUCK

DID YOU KNOW?

You won't believe what the first hockey pucks were made from...EW!

The first hockey games were played on ponds outside with whatever could be found. The first pucks were often **frozen** cow poop! These were replaced by wooden pucks, then lacrosse balls cut down to a square shape.

Whole lacrosse balls were often used by teams until the game moved indoors. By 1885, most teams were using a "hockey puck" very similar to the ones used today.

DID YOU KNOW?

The term "hockey puck" was first used on February 7, 1876.

The hockey puck is sometimes called the disk, the rubber, or the biscuit. Dedicated hockey fans are sometimes called puckheads!

The word "puck" was used for the first time in an article in the *Montreal Gazette*. These pucks were cut square, and they looked like a brick of barbeque charcoal. Today's pucks are made out of **vulcanized rubber.**

SUPER STICKS

DID YOU KNOW?

The first hockey sticks are believed to have been made, and sold, by Indigenous Canadians.

Records show that the Mi'kmaq people enjoyed playing games similar to hockey as far back as the 1700s. They made sticks from a single piece of hardwood. The Mi'kmaq made and sold "Mic-Mak" hockey sticks up until the 1930s.

This photograph shows a group of Mi'kmaq in Nova Scotia, Canada, making hockey sticks around 1890.

Modern sticks are called **composite** sticks. Most are made of layers of **carbon fiber**. They are tough, but flex easily when shooting the puck.

DID YOU KNOW?

Modern hockey sticks are strong, but bend and twist easily, which lets players shoot harder.

Sticks are measured by their flex, or the ability to bend when pressure is put on them. On a hard slapshot, the stick hits the ice behind the puck, which lets the stick flex, build up power, and then release it for a powerful shot.

AT THE RINK

DID YOU KNOW?

The first indoor hockey game occurred on March 3, 1875.

On that day, two teams of 9 players each met at Victoria Skating Rink in Montreal, Quebec. Many consider this the first organized hockey game. It was advertised in the newspaper. The event was set up by James Creighton, who would go on to create the first set of hockey rules.

This painting from 1870 is titled *Skating Carnival, Victoria Rink, Montreal, QC*. Five years later, Creighton and 17 other players played the first indoor hockey game there!

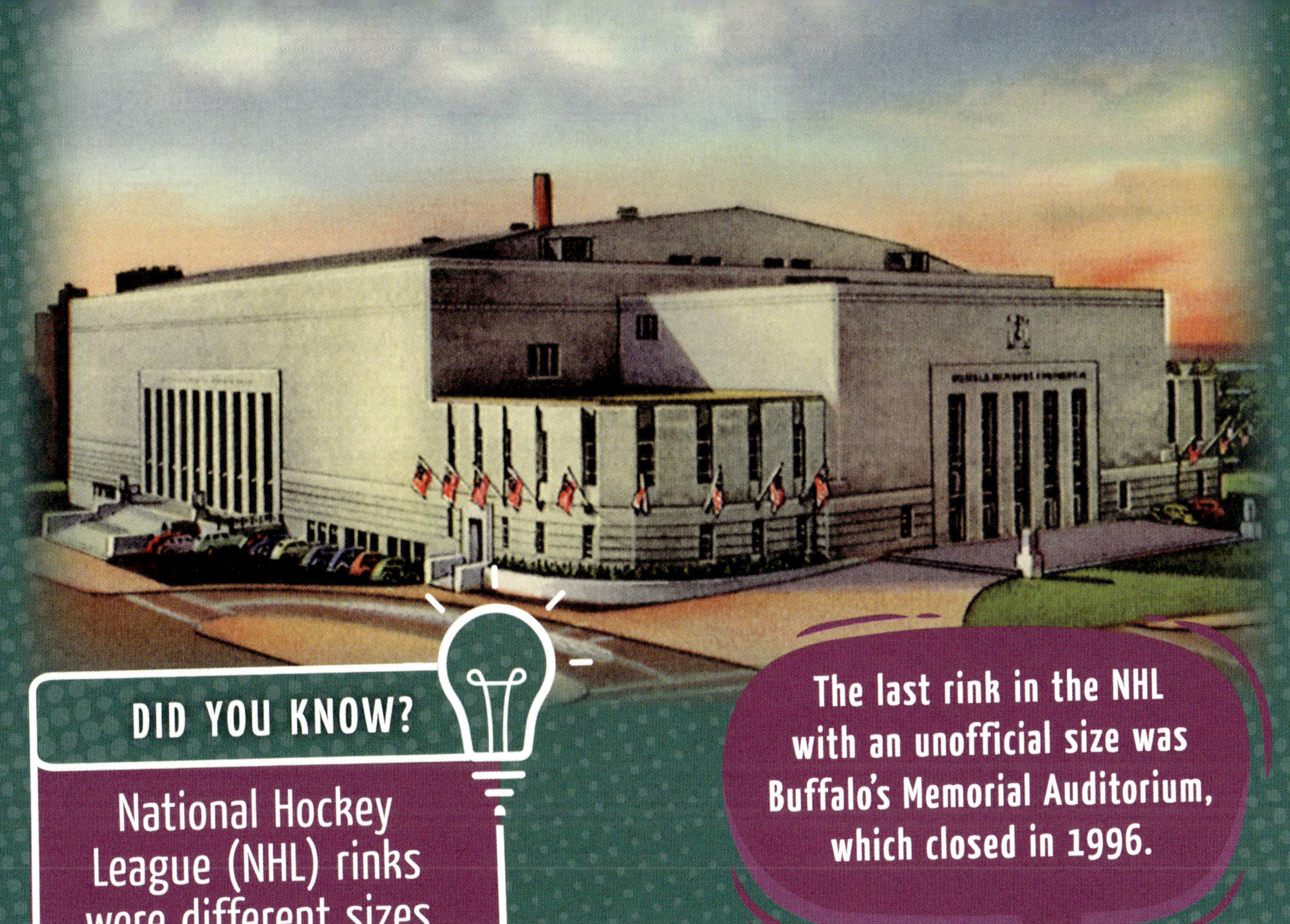

An official NHL ice rink is an oval 200 feet (61 m) long and 85 feet (26 m) wide. But not all old rinks were that size. Boston Garden, where the Bruins once played, was 191 feet by 83 feet (58 m by 25 m)!

CANADIAN TEAMS

DID YOU KNOW?

The **logo** on Toronto Maple Leafs' jerseys is much older than the maple leaf on the Canadian flag.

Toronto's first team was called the Saint Pats. In 1926, the team jersey had a green cloverleaf on them. They changed it to a blue-and-white maple leaf the next season. Canada didn't have its own maple leaf flag until 1965!

The style of the maple leaf has changed over the years.

Johnny Canuck was a comic book hero during World War II (1939–1945), and the team took the name "Canucks" to honor Canadian soldiers. The Vancouver Canucks joined the NHL in 1970.

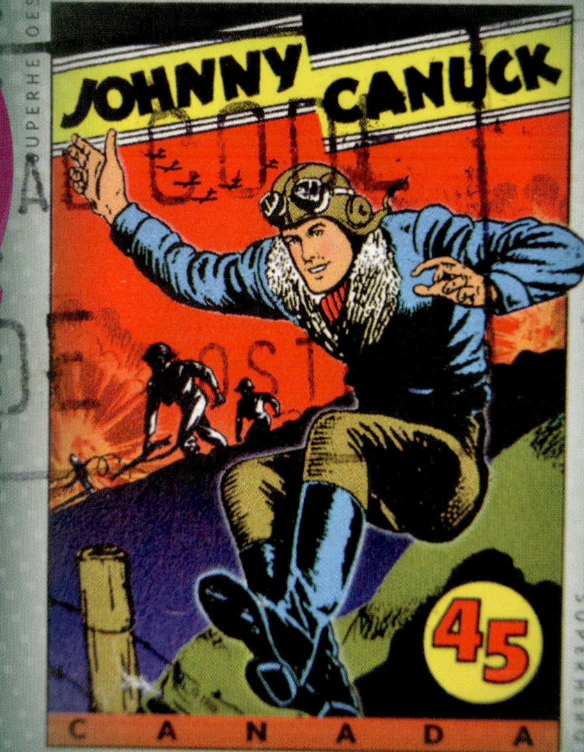

DID YOU KNOW?

Two Canadian teams in the NHL are named after Canadians.

The Montreal Canadiens are sometimes called the "Habs," which is short for "Les Habitants." That's a French term for the early French settlers in present-day Québec. The Vancouver Canucks started as part of the Pacific Coast Hockey League in 1945. "Canuck" is a slang term for a person from Canada!

THE GREAT ONE

DID YOU KNOW?

Wayne Gretzky first played pro hockey for the Indianapolis Racers.

Gretzky was signed by the Racers of the Western Hockey **Association** (WHA) In 1978. Eight games into the season, he was traded to the Edmonton Oilers, who joined the NHL the following season when the WHA folded.

In addition to the Oilers, Gretzky also played for the Los Angeles Kings, the New York Rangers, and the St. Louis Blues. Gretzky was a coach for the Pheonix Coyotes from 2005 to 2009.

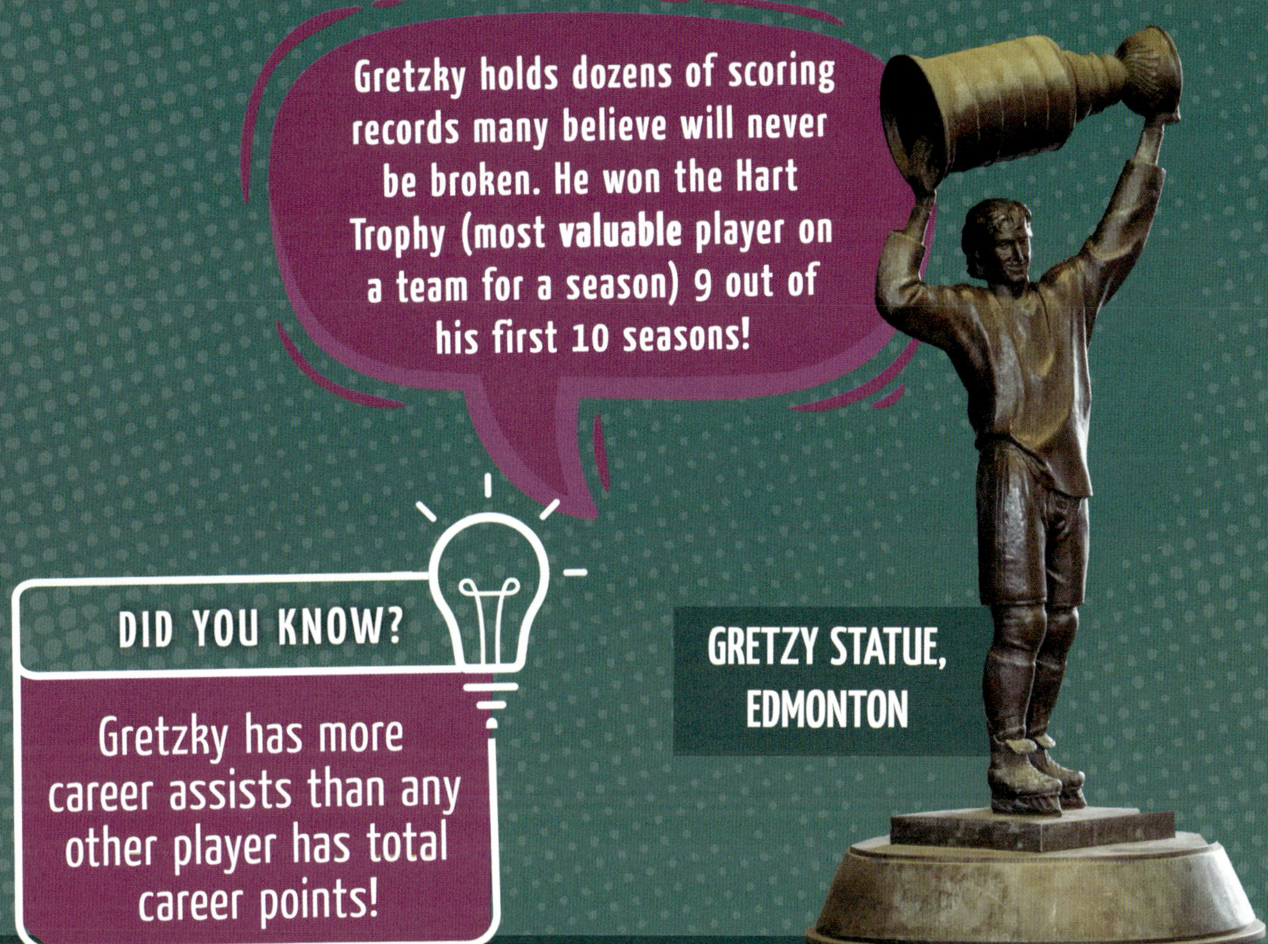

GRETZY STATUE, EDMONTON

Gretzky is first all-time in assists (1,963), and points (2,857) in NHL history. Jaromír Jágr of the Czeck Republic is second all-time in points, with "only" 1,921. Gretzky also holds the record for most goals (92), assists (163), and points (215) in a season.

THE DOMINATOR

DID YOU KNOW?

Dominik Hašek was feared by other teams and truly earned the nickname "The Dominator."

As a Buffalo Sabre in the 1996–1997 and 1997–1998 seasons, Hašek won the Vezina Trophy for best goaltender, the Hart Memorial Trophy as the league's most valuable player (MVP), and the Lester B. Pearson Award for the player voted most outstanding by other players. He later won two Stanley Cups with the Detroit Red Wings, in 2002 and 2008.

Hašek was often called a "flopper" for diving for pucks and making saves other goalies would surely have missed.

HAŠEK DOMINATES

Won Vezina Trophy 6 times for best goaltender

Led league in shutouts 6 times

Led league in save percentage for 6 straight seasons

1998 Olympic Games best goaltender

Holds record for highest career save percentage (.922)

Won Pearson Award 2 times for players' MVP

Won Hart Memorial Trophy 2 times for league MVP

Won Jennings Trophy 3 times for fewest goals allowed

Played in 6 All-Star games

IT'S A FAMILY THING

DID YOU KNOW?

For the Howe family, hockey was a group effort...sometime on the same team!

Gordie Howe, "Mr. Hockey," played 32 pro seasons in the NHL. His brother Victor played too. In 1973—two years after retiring—Gordie signed with the WHA's Houston Aeros along with his sons, Marty and Mark. The 45-year-old Howe won league MVP, and Mark was named Rookie of the Year!

The three Howes led Houston to WHA championships in 1974 and 1975.

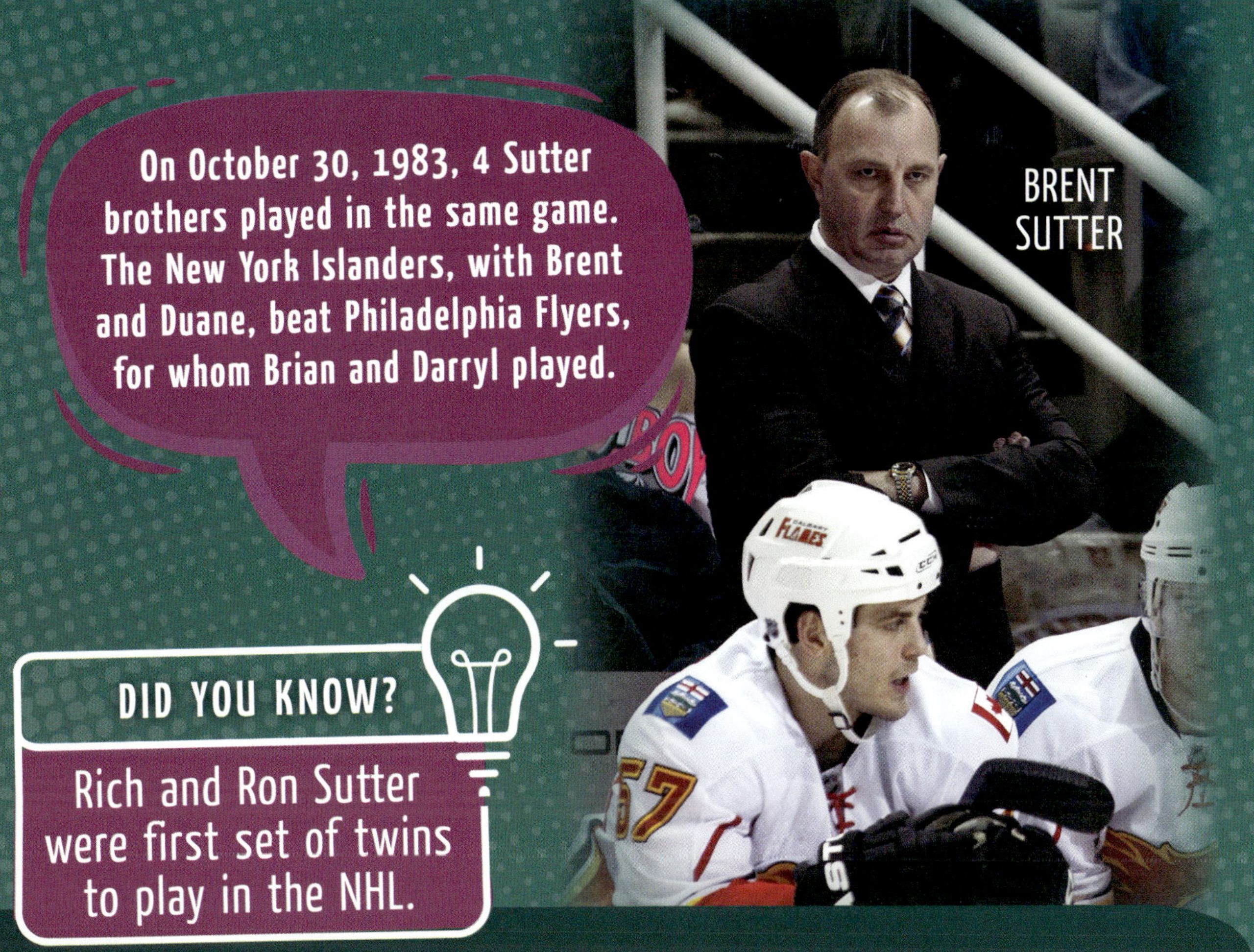

Six brothers—Brent, Brian, Darryl, Duane, Rich, and Ron—have all spent time in the NHL, winning championships as players and coaches. Three of the Sutter brothers' sons—Brandon, Brett, and Brody—have also played in the NHL, and Lukas Sutter was drafted by the Islanders in 2014.

OW, MY FACE!

DID YOU KNOW?

The first player to regularly wear a face mask was goalie Jaques Plante.

During a game in 1959, a puck hit Montreal Canadiens goalie Plante in the face and broke his nose. Plante returned wearing a face mask of his own design (shown here). The Canadiens beat the New York Rangers 3–1. After that, Plante kept wearing the mask.

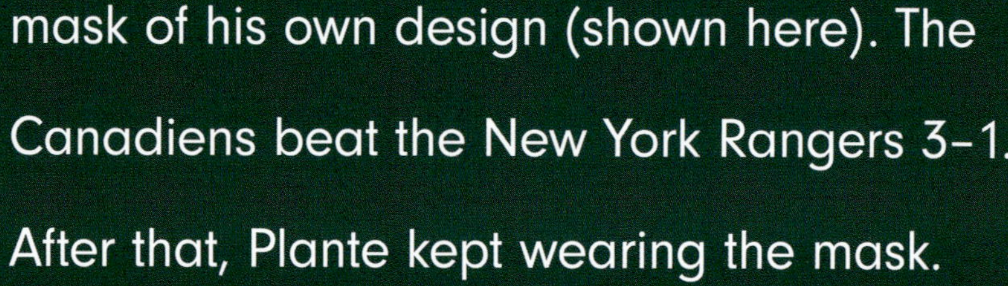

A hockey puck can hit speeds higher than 100 miles (161 km) per hour. Facial injuries and missing teeth, often called "chicklets" in the world of hockey, were once considered part of the game!

The last NHL goaltender to play without a mask was Andy Brown in 1974. Brown then played in the WHA for three seasons and still refused to wear a mask. He earned the nickname "Fearless."

DID YOU KNOW?

NHL goalies did not officially have to wear helmets and face masks until 1979!

Goalie face masks became more popular after Plante donned one. However, goalies didn't even need to wear helmets until 1979, when it became a rule. This rule states: "It is **compulsory** for all goalkeepers to wear helmets and full face masks."

FINALLY... THE FINALS!

DID YOU KNOW?

A player once killed a bat during the Stanley Cup Finals.

In 1975, Buffalo Sabres forward Jim Lorentz swatted at a bat flying around inside Buffalo Memorial Auditorium before a faceoff during Game 3 of the Finals against Philadelphia. The stick hit the bat and killed it! Lorentz got the nickname "Batman" from the incident.

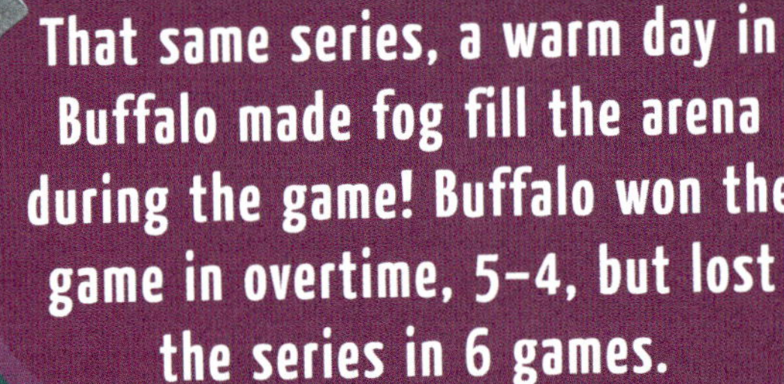

That same series, a warm day in Buffalo made fog fill the arena during the game! Buffalo won the game in overtime, 5–4, but lost the series in 6 games.

The 2019–2020 season was suspended due to the COVID-19 pandemic. The Stanley Cup Finals, usually played in late May or early June, were postponed until August when the Tampa Bay Lightning beat the Dallas Stars 4 games to 2.

The Stanley Cup Finals once ended in a tie due to the Spanish flu!

The 1919 Stanley Cup Finals between the Montreal Canadiens and Seattle Metropolitans ended after five games without a winner decided. Both teams won two games each and tied another. Game six was supposed to decide the series, but Montreal didn't have enough healthy players to play!

THE STANELY CUP

DID YOU KNOW?

The Stanley Cup was named after a Canadian politician.

Lord Stanley of Preston, or Frederick Arthur Stanley, was the Governor General of Canada in 1892. He bought a small cup for about $50 at the time and made it a **challenge trophy**. The team that held it would lose it if they lost a challenge.

In 1893, the Montreal Amateur Athletic Association (MAAA) became the first team to win the Stanley Cup.

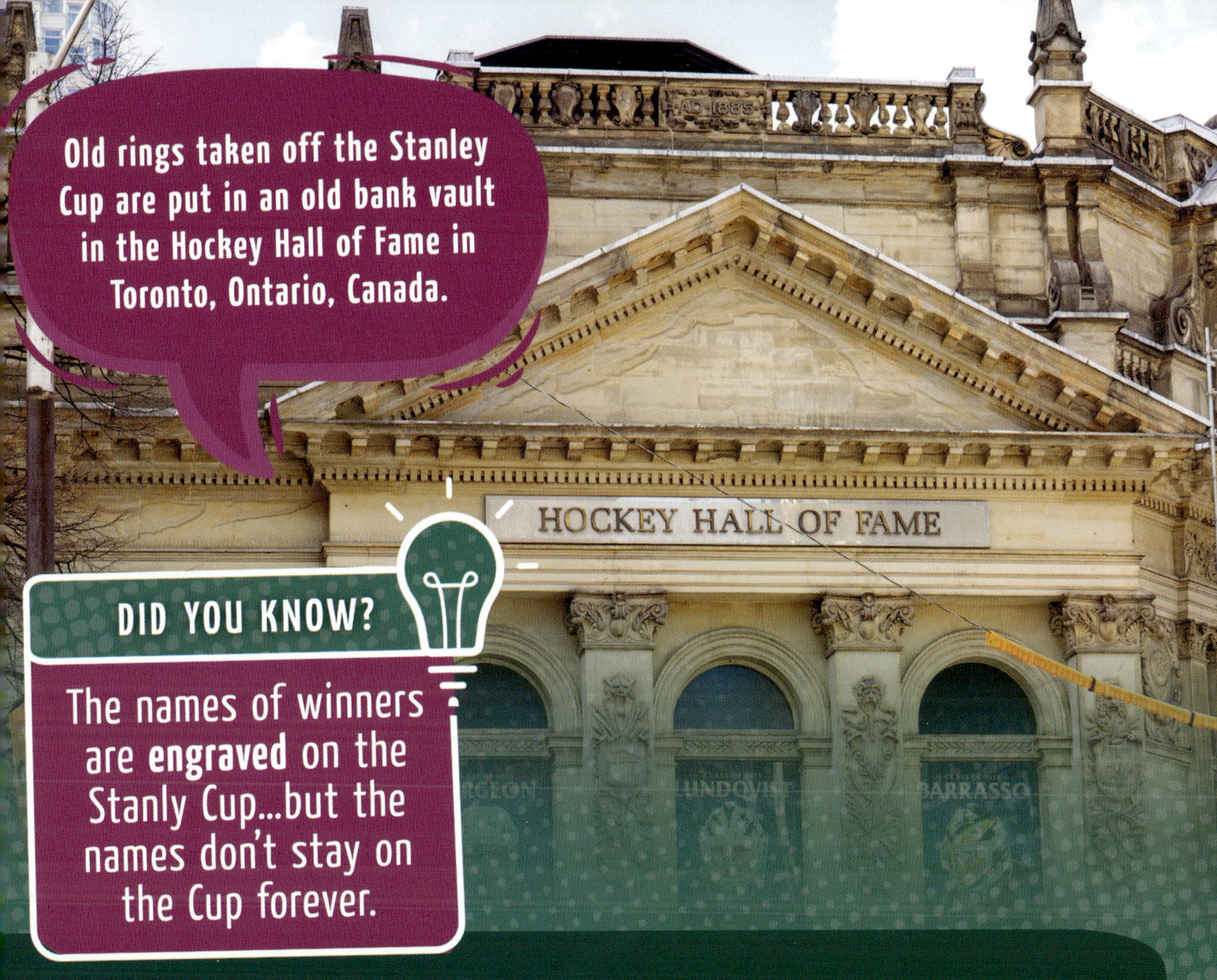

DID YOU KNOW?

The names of winners are **engraved** on the Stanly Cup...but the names don't stay on the Cup forever.

Over the years, new bands were added to the Cup to fit more winners' names. When the bands of silver on the Stanley Cup are full, an old ring is removed and a new, blank one is put on.

DID YOU KNOW?

There's more than one Stanley Cup!

By 1963, NHL president Clarence Campbell decided the original Stanley Cup was too old and worn. A **replica** "Presentation Cup" is given to the winning team, and a third Cup (another replica) is on display at the Hockey Hall of Fame.

The original Cup is also on display, along with the retired bands, in the Hall of Fame's bank vault in Toronto.

THE STANLEY CUP'S RINGS

WINNING THE CUP

The Stanley Cup itself has gone on many adventures! Winning teams get to keep the trophy for a short period. It's seen the bottom of swimming pools and once got lost in the Ottawa Canal. People even eat or drink out of it! In 1907, the Montreal Wanderers left it at a photographer's home. The photographer's mother was using it as a flowerpot when they came back for it!

The Stanley Cup is just part of hockey's fun history. Every player who wins it gets to spend a day with the big silver trophy. What would you do on your day with the Cup?

Each year, the Stanley Cup champions take the Cup on a parade through the winning city. Then the players each get their own day with the Cup later that summer.

GLOSSARY

association: A group of teams playing the same sport.

carbon fiber: A manmade fiber that has small carbon threads in it.

challenge trophy: An award that is held by a winning team but can be won by another if the holding team loses.

championship: A contest held to determine the overall winner.

composite: Made up of many different kinds of matter.

compulsory: Necessary.

engrave: To cut letters or designs on a hard metal.

frozen: Made solid by the cold.

logo: A design that is used to represent a person, company, or team.

pandemic: An illness that affects many people over a large area.

replica: A close copy of something.

valuable: Important.

vulcanized rubber: Rubber that has gone through a chemical process to make it stronger.

FOR MORE INFORMATION

BOOKS

Anderson, Josh. *Sidney Crosby vs. Wayne Gretzky: Who Would Win?* Minneapolis, MN: Learner Publishing, 2024.

Streeter, Anthony. *Stanley Cup All-Time Greats.* Mendota Heights, MN: Press Box Books, 2024.

WEBSITES

Hockey Reference
hockey-reference.com
Find stats and more about your favorite hockey players and teams here.

National Hockey League
NHL.com
Find out more about each NHL team on the league's official site.

USA Hockey
usahockey.com
Learn more about how you can start playing hockey here.

Publisher's note to educators and parents: Our editors have carefully reviewed these websites to ensure that they are suitable for students. Many websites change frequently, however, and we cannot guarantee that a site's future contents will continue to meet our high standards of quality and educational value. Be advised that students should be closely supervised whenever they access the internet.

INDEX